This book is dedicated to Rob, Natasha,
Ishmael, and Isaiah for always knowing
that "Somebody got it!"
the future is bright!

- Nicole

OH YOUR MONEY WILL GROW

This book is a **hope** and a **wish** and a **confirmation** that the person receiving it already knows they are on the right track and surrounded by great support . It is meant to be a conversation starter on all things money and time: two key items most would like in abundance! It is the opposite of a cautionary tale. It is a peek forward with a leaning toward preparation. It is what I wish I knew when I moved into adulting. If you start early....
Oh, your money... it will grow!

Oh your money
will grow, yes indeed.
Start Investing wisely,
planting the seed.

to ensure success,
you have to be wise!
Pay close attention!
Keep your eye on
the prize!

As you move through life's journey, well... you will need money!

With any job,
consider a retirement
plan.
With employer matching,
you'll be a fan!

With a trusted advisor,
you're sure to win!

Stay informed!
keep up with the market trends.
But don't panic sell,
that's where
trouble begins!

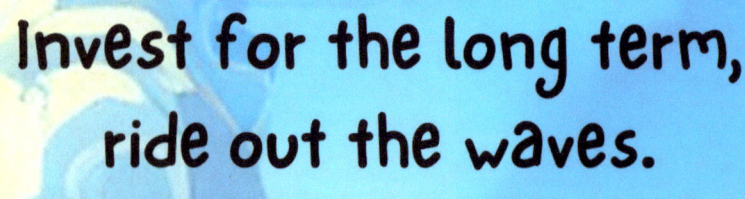

Invest for the long term,
ride out the waves.

Your money will grow,
in so many ways!

ATM LOAN

With a growing bank account, you'll make a stand!

As you navigate the world of finance and wealth,

Remember to enjoy your life, and take care of your health!

With smart choices and
patience,
you'll go far.
Invest in your future,
be a financial star!